The Groovy Green Kitchen: Volume One

Weeknight Veggie Slow Cooker

Comfort Main Dishes with Quick and Easy Sides

Geraldine Helen Hartman

The Groovy Green Slow Cooker (Volume 1)

Weeknight Veggie Slow Cooker

Comfort Main Dishes with Quick and Easy Sides

All text, recipes and cover photo:

Copyright © 2013 Geraldine Helen Hartman

ISBN-13: 978-1491263266
ISBN-10: 1491263261

Also available in eBook version.

On the cover:

Moroccan Vegetable Stew with Fragrant Orange Basmati Rice

Table of Contents

The Menus

Welcome to:

The Groovy Green Kitchen- Volume One

Weeknight Veggie Slow Cooker

Comfort Main Dishes with Quick and Easy Sides

Featuring fast and fabulous vegetarian dinners from the slow-cooker, each with quick and easy side dishes providing the perfect accompaniment. Includes complete recipes with variations, menu and serving suggestions.

Meal combos that are sure to please, including…

•Mediterranean Lasagne with Quickie Vegan Caesar Salad

•Cream of Rutabaga and Nutmeg Soup with Sausage, Cheese and Thyme Muffins

•Moroccan Vegetable Stew with Fragrant Orange Basmati Rice

•Old-Fashioned "Meaty" Stew with Parsley Dumplings

…and many more.

Weeknights are busy enough without having the hassle of time-consuming, stressful dinner preparations.

The Groovy Green Kitchen: Weeknight Veggie Slow Cooker, Comfort Main Dishes with Quick and Easy Sides provides you with hearty, kid-approved recipes that will simplify dinner, without compromising taste or nutrition.

Recipes that will please everyone at your table, even the meat-eaters! Great for family dinners and special enough when company is coming too. Weeknight dinners just got a whole lot easier and yummier! :<)

Let's get started!

Dedication

With gratitude and love to Joe, my favorite recipe

tester and keen-eyed proof-reader.

Thanks for helping with this culinary adventure!

About the Author

Geraldine Helen Hartman is an award-winning cookbook author, vegetarian cooking instructor and all-around avid foodie.

Her recipes and food articles have been featured in numerous publications and at websites including:

The Meatless Monday Campaign, The Veggie Table, The Cooking News, The Pennsylvania Mercury, Carolina Woman Magazine, The Indiana Gazette, The City Hippie, Savvy Vegetarian and many more.

In addition to her love of all things from the kitchen, Geraldine is a freelance writer, artisan, poet and avid blogger. She recently completed her first novel: **Third Chapter, Second Chance** and is now working on a sequel.

Other projects in progress include the second installment in

The Groovy Green Kitchen series:

Simply, Super, Supper Soups

(see last pages for a sample recipe).

Visit Geraldine's cooking, craft and cat blog:

Veggies, Yarns & Tails

Check out all her books and eBooks at:

Amazon author page for Geraldine Helen Hartman

Read this First

Some Suggestions, Tips and Time-Savers

You Won't Want to Miss!

Slow Cooker Tips:

-Slow Cooker Sizes. Recipes in this collection were all made in a 6 Quart slow cooker.

I use the <u>Hamilton Beach Set & Forget Deluxe 6 Qt. Slow Cooker</u> and have had consistently good results.

If you are just in the process of buying your first slow cooker, get one that is at least a 5-6 quart capacity, preferably 6 quart.

One of the best things about using a slow cooker is being able to make enough food for 6-8 servings. This can also mean "cooking once, enjoying twice" if you are only feeding 2-4 people.

If you plan to buy two slow cookers, it's handy to have a smaller 3-4 quart size for recipes such as: sauces, side dishes and some desserts.

-One of the first things I had to learn when I started to use my slow cooker on a regular basis was to curb my habit of lifting the lid while food was cooking, to check and stir. Don't lift the lid while food is cooking in the slow cooker unless absolutely necessary. Every time the lid is removed, you lower the cooking temperature and may add to overall cooking time. When using a slow cooker, frequent stirring is not required or recommended. Set it and for the most part, forget it; until you're ready to enjoy your culinary creation!

-Always combine ingredients thoroughly before you start the cooking process and stir only when adding additional ingredients to slow cooker, if at all possible.

-Unless stated otherwise, all recipes are cooked with the lid on, throughout the cooking process. And do insure that the lid is securely in place to provide a good seal, not slightly ajar at any time during the cooking process.

-The clips on the sides of some slow cookers are only for transporting food if required. Not required during the actual cooking process, unless stated otherwise in your slow cooker manual. And speaking of manuals, do take a few minutes to read through yours, before starting to use your slow cooker for the first time. I usually pick up at least one or two helpful tips in any product manual!

-Various brands and types of slow cookers will each give slightly different results when it comes to cooking times required. Experiment with your own slow cooker and note the time/temperature yours required, for each recipe. Start with cooking times suggested in each recipe and go from there.

-When adding additional ingredients towards the end of the cooking process: thickeners, cream, sour cream…combine them with about a ½ cup of the cooking liquid before stirring into the rest of the ingredients. This helps to bring the temperature back up more quickly after lid is replaced.

-I use a "sauté and steam" method in most of my slow cooker recipes and many others too, to optimize flavours. This is my personal variation of a cooking tip that I learned many years ago from one of Canada's most celebrated chefs: **Pol Martin**. Some slow cooker recipes suggest just adding vegetables, spices etc… to the slow cooker, without any precooking. What you will usually end up with is less than optimal flavours. I'm all for saving dishes and time but this quick and easy "sauté and steam" step really is worth the small extra effort.

One of the comments that I've heard consistently over the years about many of my soup, stew and main dish recipes has been the exceptional flavors people have noted when using them. I credit this simple cooking tip, for these consistently flavorful and superior results. Don't skip this step!

-Slow cooking draws out the water content in many vegetables and fruits, especially sweet peppers, adding to the final amount of liquid you will have at the end of cooking time. Don't add more water or stock than suggested in recipe until cooking is almost completed. You probably won't need to!

-When using frozen vegetables in the slow cooker, always partially thaw (20-30 minutes) before adding to other ingredients, so that cooking temperature can quickly be reached or is back up to what it should be.

-Unless otherwise stated, use dried herbs in slow cooker recipes. Dried herbs stand up well to the long, slow cooking process and retain their flavor better than fresh herbs. Exception: For garnishes, definitely go with fresh parsley and other herbs, for a burst of flavor and color.

Buy small quantities of the herbs and spices that you don't use on a regular basis, to keep them fresh and flavorful.

Miscellaneous Cooking Tips:

-Abbreviations used in this book:

C = 1 cup/ 8 ounces, T =1 level tablespoon, teas. = 1 level teaspoon. Use proper measuring spoons not cutlery, for accurate measures.

-When a range for amount of ingredient to use is given, start with lowest amount suggested when in doubt and then adjust to taste and note your preferences for next time. Using spices and herbs is a lot of fun and it's all about personal preferences. Experiment, it's one of the true joys of cooking!

-Use **certified** organic ingredients. So worth the slight extra cost. And with the popularity of organics growing by leaps and bounds, the price gap for organic vs. non-organic products is getting smaller and smaller. For your health, for superior taste, for the environment, for so many good reasons: choose certified organic ingredients whenever possible.

-When pureeing cream soups, remove slow cooker lid and allow ingredients to cool slightly before blending to desired consistency. And do invest in an immersion blender if you don't already have one. So handy, especially when processing a large batch of soup in the slow cooker and with stovetop soup cooking too.

-When using garlic in a recipe, mince/dice/slice… the garlic first when prepping several vegetables to allow garlic's healthful, medicinal ingredients to become active. Read more about garlic's numerous health benefits online.

-Buying and preparing beans. I use precooked beans in all my recipes, I do not recommend using canned beans, unless you are pressed for time and they are the only option available. If using canned beans, make sure to rinse in cold water thoroughly and drain well, before using in recipes.

Preparing beans from dry form is quick and easy, with a bit of preplanning.

Allow ½ the amount of dry beans for the precooked beans required. For example: if a recipe calls for 4 C. of precooked beans, start with 2 C. dry.

Buy beans from a store that sells them on a fairly quick basis; even dry beans can become stale and tasteless.

Thoroughly rinse beans in cold water, removing any discolored ones at the same time. After rinsing, cover beans with fresh cold water, allowing a couple of inches of water above beans in the container. Cover and allow to soak in the refrigerator overnight.

Drain thoroughly, place beans in cooking pot and cover with cold water, again allowing a couple of inches of water above the beans. You can add a couple of bay leaves and/or a vegetable soup cube if desired. The bay leaves are supposed to help with "gas" issues. The vegetable soup cube, to add flavor. Both are optional.

Cover and bring beans to a rapid boil. Reduce heat and simmer for 30 minutes. Turn off heat, leave on burner and allow beans to continue to soften for an additional 30 minutes. For most beans, this is adequate time to precook beans to a perfect consistency; not mushy but cooked through.

Navy beans will require a bit more cooking time, 40-45 minutes of simmering instead of 30 minutes.

-Dicing/Chopping ingredients. When using a slow cooker, it's even more important to cut ingredients to a uniform size to insure even cooking.

When dicing follow these guidelines:

Minced- Dice as finely as possible and then press with the side of a large cutting knife to reduce even more. Don't overdo or you'll end up with a paste (ie: when mincing garlic)

Finely diced- cut into squares, less than ¼"

Diced- cut into ¼- ½" squares

Coarsely diced- cut into ½" - ¾" squares

When a recipe calls for chopped ingredients, cutting to exact sizes is not as crucial or specific. Use your personal preferences when it comes to chopped foods. Finely chopped is usually suggested for herbs for garnishes and this is a good rule to follow.

-Dairy vs. Non-Dairy Milk products. I try to limit my use/consumption of dairy products and have had good success using plain soy milk and vegan-type sour cream, in many recipes. There are also many other non-dairy milk products now available including: rice, almond, hemp, coconut. Experiment to find your own particular favorite, if you prefer to use non-dairy milk products.

Sour cream: I do add it to a number of recipes to add richness and flavor. A little goes a long way so the calories/fat content can be worth it.

Butter vs. Margarine: The health debate continues when it comes to these ingredients. If you do wish to use margarine, buy non-whipped, good quality margarine preferably organic. I use Earth Balance Organic and have had good results, especially when baking with it.

-Meat substitutes. I try to limit my use of all types of processed foods. But sometimes the flavor benefits are worth adding a product like non-meat sausages to a recipe. I use Tofurky Beer Brats in many of my recipes. They are spicy and flavorful but do have a rather high sodium content so no additional salt is required when adding these to a recipe. When using any type of meat substitutes, do check out the ingredient list and processing procedures carefully.

Read more online about veggie burger choices and what to look for and to beware of, when choosing a brand.

You can also check out my product review blog:

www.myreallifereviews.com

for reports on this topic and product reviews of some of the (bolded) ingredients used in the recipes.

Baking and Bread Machine Tips

-Using a bread machine can be a quick and easy way to enjoy fresh homemade bread on a regular basis. Use these tips to insure consistently good results.

While the dough is in the mixing phase, check to insure that the dough is forming a smooth, non-sticky ball as you would for a scratch loaf of bread. It's ok to lift the lid during the mixing phase but not while the loaf is rising or baking. Add a bit more flour or room temperature water (1 T. at a time) if required, to achieve a smooth ball of dough, that moves easily inside the bread machine pan.

I use Traditional dry yeast for my bread machine recipes and have had consistently good results, with no over-rising. Experiment to find the type of yeast that works best for you. This can vary depending on the altitude where you live and the room temperature when you are making bread. If rapid rise bread machine yeast works better for you, by all means use it!

-Biscuits and Scones. When preparing biscuit/scone dough, handle as little as possible, to insure a light, pleasing texture when biscuits are baked. Less is more.

Add just enough additional flour as required, to form a soft but smooth dough, again don't overdo.

Mediterranean Lasagne with Quickie Vegan Caesar Salad

Mediterranean Lasagne

An intriguing and delectable variation of an old family favourite. If you've never used your slow cooker for making lasagne before, you're in for a real treat. No more crusty, burnt edges; just yummy perfection, every time. Serves 6.

12 oz. marinated artichoke hearts (drain and reserve marinade)

3 C. tomato sauce mixed with 1 C. water

2 T. tomato paste

2 T. reserved marinade

500 gr. regular or low-fat Ricotta cheese

2 C. coarsely shredded fresh Swiss chard or spinach

2 T. olive oil

2 medium onions, diced

4-6 cloves garlic, minced (to taste)

3 medium zucchini, cut in ½" circles

1 T. Italian seasoning blend OR ½ T. dried crushed oregano
and ½ T. dried crushed basil leaves

1 C. finely-shredded Mozzarella cheese

½ C. grated Parmesan cheese

9 oven-ready lasagne noodles (don't precook)

1 teas. butter or margarine for greasing slow-cooker liner.

Finely chop the drained artichokes and set aside.

In a medium-sized bowl, combine tomato sauce and water,
tomato paste and 2 T. reserved artichoke marinade. Set
aside.

In a medium-sized bowl, combine Ricotta cheese and Swiss
chard. Set aside.

In a small bowl, combine Mozzarella and Parmesan cheese

and set aside.

In a large skillet or Dutch oven, heat olive oil over MEDIUM heat. Add onions and garlic and sauté for 2 minutes. Add zucchini and Italian seasoning mix and sauté 1 additional minute. Stir in the tomato sauce mixture. Remove from heat and set aside.

Thoroughly grease slow-cooker liner with butter or margarine.

Layer as follows: evenly spreading each layer, to outer edges of slow cooker liner:

Begin with 1/3 of the tomato/vegetable sauce mixture. Layer with 3 lasagne noodles (break in half if necessary to fit), then a layer of the Ricotta/Swiss chard mixture. Top with another 1/3 of the tomato/vegetable sauce mixture and 3 more noodles.

Layer with all of the artichokes.

Layer with remaining Ricotta/Parmesan mix and 3 lasagne noodles. Top with Mozzarella/Parmesan mix and finish with remaining tomato/vegetable sauce mixture to complete layers.

Cook on HIGH for 3 hours or LOW for 6 hours. Allow to set 5 minutes (uncovered) before cutting and serving.

Variation: Gluten-free version. Substitute brown rice lasagne noodles for the oven-ready kind.

Pre-cook noodles: In a large pot of salted, boiling water cook noodles for 1 minute (don't overcook!). Remove from heat, drain, gently rinse with cold water and drain again. Set aside to cool in a colander until ready to use.

Noodles should be only slightly softened after par-boiling so that they aren't mushy in the completed recipe.

Check tomato sauce and artichokes for any gluten content.

Gluten-free version is best cooked on HIGH to keep noodles from getting too soft when cooking time is complete.

Quickie Vegan Caesar Salad

Caesar salad goes perfectly with most types of pasta dishes. This one is quick to make, with the added crunch and nutritional boost of sunflower seeds. Vegan- friendly too. Omit the croutons if you want to make it gluten-free.

Serves 4-6.

Salad:

3 Romaine lettuce hearts or one large Romaine lettuce

½ large red onion, thinly sliced in rings

½ C. hulled raw sunflower seeds

1 C. Kalamata or green olives of choice, left whole or sliced

Croutons: (optional)

2 large slices crusty bread of choice (day old works best), cut in 1" cubes

1 T. minced garlic

1 T. Italian seasoning blend OR ½ T. dried crushed oregano
and ½ T. dried crushed basil leaves

2 T. olive oil

Dressing:

3/4 C. vegan-type mayonnaise (store-bought or homemade)

2 T. extra-virgin olive oil

1-2 teas. **Mrs. Dash Original Blend** seasoning (to taste)

¼- ½ teas. freshly ground black pepper (to taste)

½- 1 teas. sea salt (to taste, optional)

If not including croutons add:

2 T. fresh thyme, finely chopped

1 T. minced garlic

Garnishes:

1 large lemon, cut in wedges

1 C. finely grated fresh Parmesan or Asiago cheese

Tear lettuce into large, bite-sized pieces, discarding any

yellowish leaves. Thoroughly wash and dry lettuce and place in a large salad bowl.

Layer with onion rings, sunflower seeds and olives and set aside.

Optional croutons:

Preheat oven or toaster oven to 375F. In a small bowl, combine crouton ingredients. Place on an ungreased baking sheet and bake for 15-20 minutes, until crunchy and slightly browned; turning once after 10 minutes. Watch that they don't overbrown. Cool to room temperature and add to salad.

Combine dressing ingredients. Drizzle over salad just before serving, tossing salad gently to combine all ingredients.

Garnish with lemon wedges and grated cheese. Enjoy!

Sweet Red Pepper and Salsa Soup with Toaster Oven Focaccia

Sweet Red Pepper and Salsa Soup

A flavorful, brilliantly- colored cream soup. Perfect for any meal, even an elegant, company dinner. Serves 4-6.

Note: Sweet red peppers have a lot of water in them and will add to the total volume of this soup as they cook.

3 T. olive oil

4 large sweet red peppers, coarsely diced

1 large sweet onion, coarsely diced

2-4 cloves of garlic, minced (to taste)

½- 1 T. crushed dried thyme leaves (to taste)

¼- ½ teas. freshly ground- pepper (to taste)

¼- ½ teas. sea salt (to taste, optional)

1 T. cornstarch

4 T. tomato salsa (mild or medium)

3 C. vegetable soup stock

½ C. light or regular sour cream

Garnish: Finely chopped fresh parsley

In a large skillet or Dutch oven, heat olive oil over MEDIUM-HIGH heat. Add red peppers, onion and garlic and sauté for 5 minutes. Stir in spices. Cover, reduce heat to

MEDIUM and steam for 5 minutes to release flavours.
Transfer to slow cooker.

Stir in cornstarch, dredging all vegetables evenly. Add all
remaining ingredients **except sour cream.**

Cook on HIGH for 3 hours or LOW for 6 hours, **adding
sour cream** for last 10 minutes of cooking time on HIGH.

Remove from heat and allow soup to cool slightly.

Using an immersion blender, puree to desired consistency.
Reheat slightly if required.

Garnish and serve.

Toaster-Oven Focaccia (with choice of toppings)

A wonderful addition with almost any kind of soup or stew dinner and so much better and fresher than the pricey, store-bought varieties. Focaccia bread has a wonderful, chewy texture with a slightly crisp crust. Great for sandwiches too. Bakes perfectly in a large toaster-oven or use a conventional range if desired.

3/4 C. warm water

2 teas. Traditional dry yeast

1 teas. raw sugar

2 ½ -3 C. unbleached white flour

½ teas. sea salt

Extra-virgin olive oil

In a large bowl, combine warm water, yeast and sugar. Stir to combine, cover and set aside for 15-20 minutes until yeast is completely dissolved and foamy.

Combine flour (start with 2 ½ C.) and salt and gradually add to the first mixture to form a soft dough. Add a bit more flour if required.

Knead on a floured board for about 5 minutes until dough forms a nice, smooth ball.

Wash and dry mixing bowl previously used, grease thoroughly with olive oil and place dough into bowl, turning over to oil all sides. Cover with a damp tea towel and allow to rise for about 1 hour, until doubled in volume.

Punch down dough and knead for 1 minute.

Lightly oil (use olive oil) a 9 ½ x 11" or 8 x 12" metal baking pan (with a rim).

Spread dough out on pan to outer edges, keeping thickness throughout as even as possible.

Top with **desired toppings (see below**) and allow to rise (uncovered) in a warm place for 30-40 minutes, until doubled.

10 minutes before end of rising time, preheat oven to 450F for toaster-oven or conventional range, on convection setting if available and with oven rack at lowest position.

Bake 10-12 minutes until slightly golden on top. Reduce

heat to 425F after first 5 minutes, if browning too fast.

Toppings:

Basic: Drizzle dough with 3 T. olive oil and sprinkle with medium-grind sea salt (to taste) before rising.

Basic Savory: Drizzle dough with 3 T. olive oil and sprinkle with medium-grind sea salt and freshly ground black pepper (to taste) before rising.

Cheesy-Italian: Drizzle dough with 3 T. olive oil and sprinkle with 1 C. finely grated fresh Parmesan cheese, 1 teas. **Mrs. Dash Original Blend** seasoning and 2 teas. crushed dried oregano leaves or Italian seasoning blend, before rising.

Sunny Paris: Drizzle dough with 3 T. olive oil and sprinkle with 1-2 T. **Sunny Paris** salt-free seasoning from the Spice House (a wonderful and unique flavor blend!)

Pesto: Spread 4 T. basil pesto over dough before rising.

Greek: Drizzle dough with 3 T. olive oil and top with 1 teas. crushed dried thyme leaves, 2 teas. crushed dried oregano leaves and 1 C. thinly-sliced green or black olives.

Whole Grain: Substitute 1 C. whole wheat flour for 1 C. of the unbleached white flour.

Marvelous Mulligatawny Soup with Sunflower and Oat Bread Machine Bread

Marvelous Mulligatawny Soup

My version of the classic East Indian vegetable and fruit soup. Flavorful, colorful and oh so hearty. A meal-in-a-bowl your family will love. Serves 6-8.

2 large unpeeled sweet red apples, diced

1 T. fresh lemon juice

3 T. olive oil

2 medium onions, diced

5 cloves of garlic, minced

3 large carrots, cut in ½" thick circles

3 large stalks of celery, diced

1 C. diced rutabaga

1-2 T. curry paste: mild, medium or hot (to taste)

1 T. crushed, dried thyme leaves

1/4-1/2 teas. freshly-ground black pepper (to taste)

½ - 1 teas. sea salt, (to taste, optional)

2 bay leaves (remove before serving)

2 C. chickpeas (precooked or if using canned, thoroughly

rinsed and drained)

6 C. vegetable soup stock

1 large green pepper, finely diced

Garnish: Finely-chopped fresh parsley

Combine diced apple with lemon juice in a small bowl (to
avoid discolouration) and set aside.

In a large skillet or Dutch oven, heat olive oil over
MEDIUM-HIGH heat. Add onions, garlic, carrots, celery,
rutabaga and apple with lemon juice. Stir to combine
thoroughly and sauté for 5 minutes.

Add curry paste and spices. Cover, reduce heat to
MEDIUM and steam for 5 minutes to release flavours.

Transfer to slow cooker. Add all remaining ingredients

except the green pepper. Stir to combine thoroughly.

Cook on HIGH for 3 ½ hours or LOW for 7 hours,

adding green pepper for last 20 minutes of cooking time

on HIGH.

Adjust seasonings if required.

Garnish with parsley and serve.

Sunflower and Oat Bread Machine Bread

A delicious and versatile, basic bread recipe.

Great for sandwiches, toast or on its own with spread(s) of choice.

1 C. boiling water

½ C. regular rolled oats

2 T good-quality, non-whipped margarine or butter

2 T. honey

1 T. molasses

1 large free-range egg

2 C. unbleached white flour

1 C. whole- wheat or whole- wheat/white blend flour

½ teas. sea salt

1 ½ teas. Traditional dry yeast

½ C. hulled raw sunflower seeds

In a small bowl, combine boiling water and oats. Set aside to cool to lukewarm. Add margarine or butter, honey, molasses and egg and stir to combine.

In another bowl, combine flours and salt.

Add liquid and then dry ingredients **except sunflower seeds** to bread machine, followed by the yeast (make sure not to get it wet).

Set at: WHOLE GRAIN/LIGHT or MEDIUM CRUST/1 ½ POUNDS. Start machine. **Add sunflower seeds at beep.**

Allow loaf to cool slightly before removing from pan when baking is completed.

Luscious Cheddar Scalloped Potatoes with Maple-Glazed Veggie Sausages

Luscious Cheddar Scalloped Potatoes

This recipe is the ultimate in comfort food classics!

A slow cooker is the perfect appliance for making perfect scalloped potatoes, every time. With less than 30 minutes of prep time, you'll be rewarded with a dinner sure to please! Add a dark green vegetable if you're really hungry, for a nice color contrast. Serves 4-6.

1 teas. butter or margarine for greasing slow-cooker liner.

10 medium or 8 large red-skinned potatoes, peeled and thinly sliced

2 medium onions, diced

3 T. good-quality non-whipped margarine or butter

3 T. unbleached white flour

1 ½ C. milk

2 T. Dijon mustard

¼- ½ teas. freshly-ground black pepper (to taste)

2 teas. crushed dried thyme leaves

10 oz. can low-sodium (preferred) or regular cream of mushroom soup

1 C. grated sharp Cheddar cheese

¼ teas. ground turmeric (optional but adds a nice golden color, especially if using white Cheddar)

Optional garnish: Ground paprika

Thoroughly grease slow-cooker liner with the 1 teas. butter

or margarine and set aside.

Prepare potatoes and onions. Place the potato slices in bowl of cold water until ready to assemble to prevent browning.

In a medium saucepan, melt margarine or butter over MEDIUM-LOW heat. Gradually add flour to form a roué (smooth paste).

Add the milk gradually and stir constantly, until mixture thickens slightly. Add remaining sauce ingredients, stir to combine thoroughly and continue to cook just until cheese melts. Remove from heat.

Thoroughly drain potato slices and set aside.

Spread 1/3 of sauce over bottom of prepared slow cooker

liner. Layer with 1/3 of the potatoes and ½ of the onions.

Repeat layers once more. Finish with remaining potatoes,

with sauce as the final layer on top.

Cook on HIGH for 3 ½ hours or LOW for 7 hours or until

potatoes are fork-tender but not mushy.

Remove from heat and remove cover; allow potatoes to set

for 5 minutes before serving.

Garnish each serving with a sprinkle of ground paprika if

desired.

Maple-Glazed Veggie Sausages

"Dress-up" store-bought vegan sausages with a drizzle of pure maple syrup. Steamed to perfection with just a hint of sweetness. Mmm….good!

Vegan, beer-brat-type sausages approx. 3.5 oz. each. Allow 1 or 2 per person. (I use **Tofurky** brand. These are very filling, one per person is usually enough!)

2 T. vegetable oil

Good quality pure maple syrup (allow 1 teas. per sausage)

Cut sausages into 1" chunks.

In a skillet, heat oil over MEDIUM-HIGH heat. Add sausage chunks and sauté for 1 minute. Drizzle with maple syrup and 2 T. water and stir to combine. Cover, reduce heat to MEDIUM and steam for 5 minutes.

Serve drizzled with remaining maple cooking liquid if desired.

Slow-Simmered Cabbage Rolls with Dilled Baby Carrots

Slow-Simmered Cabbage Rolls

A family favorite re-do, made easier and tastier using a slow-cooker instead of a conventional oven. No more dried- out or burnt cabbage, just perfect results every time! Serves 6.

1teas. butter or margarine for greasing slow-cooker liner

18-20 large green cabbage leaves (1 large or 2 small cabbages) Savoy or regular green cabbage both work well **Hint**: Save cabbage cores for adding to soups, stocks or making coleslaw).

2 T. white vinegar.

2 T. vegetable oil

1 large onion, finely-diced

1 large red, yellow or orange sweet pepper, finely-diced

1 vegan beer- brat sausage, finely-diced (I use **Tofurky**

brand)

2 C. precooked long-grain rice, your choice for type (I use brown Basmati rice)

4 T. basil pesto

1 C. drained, diced canned tomatoes

2 teas. **Mrs. Dash Original Blend** seasoning

2- 10 oz. cans low-sodium (preferred) or regular tomato soup (divided)

Optional garnish: Vegan or regular sour cream

Thoroughly grease slow-cooker liner with butter or margarine and set aside.

Bring a large pot of water to a boil. Add white vinegar and the cabbage leaves (do in two batches if necessary). Cover, bring water back to a boil and simmer cabbage leaves over MEDIUM-LOW heat for 5 minutes, until slightly softened.

Remove cabbage leaves from water and drain in a colander. Set aside to cool.

In a large skillet or Dutch oven, heat oil over MEDIUM-HIGH heat. Add onion, red pepper and sausage and sauté for 5 minutes. Remove from heat. Add: rice, pesto, tomatoes, Mrs. Dash seasoning and 1/2 can of the tomato soup. Stir to combine thoroughly.

Place approximately 3-4 T. of the veg-rice mixture in the center of a cabbage leaf. Pull together sides of cabbage leaf, then roll lengthwise as neatly as possible, forming a compact roll. Place cabbage rolls, side by side in the prepared slow-cooker liner, in two layers.

Continue to form cabbage rolls, using up all the cabbage leaves. **Hint:** If you have any veg-rice mixture left over, sauté lightly for a wonderful side dish or taco filling, to enjoy at another time.)

Pour remaining tomato soup over all the cabbage rolls.

Cook on HIGH for 3 ½ hours or LOW for 7 hours or until cabbage is tender but not mushy, don't overcooked.

Garnish with a small dollop of sour cream if desired.

Dilled Baby Carrots

A perfect vegetable side dish to go with these satisfying cabbage rolls and many other main dishes. Adds a brilliant burst of color to your plate too! Serves 6-8.

6 C. whole "baby" carrots

2 T. good-quality, non-whipped margarine or butter

4 T. finely chopped fresh dill

sea salt and freshly-ground pepper (to taste)

In a medium saucepan, bring 1 C. water to a boil. Add carrots, cover and cook over MEDIUM heat for 8-10 minutes (depends on size of carrots) just until carrots are fork-tender but still slightly crunchy.

Remove from heat, drain carrots and add remaining ingredients, stir to combine thoroughly.

Variation: If you have a steamer basket, bring 2" of water to a boil, under steamer basket, cover and continue instructions as above, no draining required.

Stick-to-Your- Ribs Black Bean Soup with Hearty Potato Scones

Stick-to-Your Ribs Black Bean Soup

Great for warming up and filling up a hungry crowd especially on a cold winter day. An oh, so satisfying black bean soup with a spicy kick! Serves 6-8.

Note: Peppers have a lot of water in them and will add to the total volume of this soup as they cook.

½ - 1 T. crushed, dried oregano leaves (to taste)

½ - 1 T. crushed, dried thyme leaves (to taste)

(or substitute 1-2 T. Italian seasoning blend for the oregano and thyme)

½ T. cumin seeds, crushed

2 teas. chili powder

2 teas. **Mrs. Dash Original Blend** seasoning (optional)

½ teas. sea salt (optional)

1-2 teas. raw sugar or honey (optional. add if using tomatoes that are tart)

3 T. olive oil

1 large onion, finely-diced

4-6 cloves garlic, minced (to taste)

1 large sweet red pepper, diced

1 large green pepper, diced

4 C. vegetable soup stock

28 oz. can stewed or diced tomatoes with juice

3 C. precooked black turtle beans

2 large bay leaves (remove before serving)

2 T. fresh lemon or lime juice

Optional garnish: regular or vegan sour cream.

In a small bowl or cup, combine herbs, spices and sugar (if using) and set aside.

In a large skillet or Dutch oven, heat oil over MEDIUM-

HIGH heat.

Add onions and garlic and sauté for 3-4 minutes. Add red

and green pepper and spice mix and stir to combine

ingredients thoroughly. Cover, reduce heat to MEDIUM

and steam for 5 minutes to release flavours. Transfer to slow

cooker. Add all remaining ingredients and stir to combine

thoroughly.

Cook on HIGH for 3 ½ hours or LOW for 7 hours or until

beans are very tender but not mushy.

Adjust seasonings if required.

Garnish with a small dollop of sour cream if desired.

Hearty Potato Scones

These scones are melt-in-your-mouth good and very
satisfying too. The potatoes add a unique texture and taste.
One is never enough! Makes 8 large scones.

1 ½ C. unbleached white flour

2 teas. baking powder

½ teas. sea salt

1 T. raw sugar

1/3 C. chilled butter or good-quality, non-whipped
margarine (I use **Earth Balance Organic**)

¾ C. cold mashed potatoes (a great way to use up leftovers)

½ C. (approximately, see method below) milk or soy milk

Lightly grease a baking sheet and set aside.

Combine first 4 ingredients in a large mixing bowl. Cut in
butter until crumbly. Add mashed potatoes and stir to

combine. Add just enough milk to form a soft dough.

Shape dough into a ball and allow to rest for 15 minutes on a floured board, covered with a damp dish towel.

Preheat oven to 375F while dough is rising.

Knead dough slightly for 1 minute and re-form into a ball. Place on prepared baking sheet and pat into a circle about 1" thick. Score top of circle to form 8 triangles.

Bake 20-25 minutes until golden brown. Reduce heat to 350F after first 10 minutes of baking time, if browning too fast.

Variation:

Tea-time Raisin: Add 1 C. golden Sultana raisins and increase sugar to 4 T. Add with the mashed potatoes.

Curried Lentil-Veggie Soup with Oven-

Baked Chappatis

Curried Lentil-Veggie Soup

Oh so satisfying and spiced just right. Great for chasing the "blahs" away on any day or if you're feeling a bit under the weather. Serves 6-8.

1-2 T. good quality curry powder (to taste) (Note: **Madras** type curry is very hot)

1 teas. crushed, dried thyme leaves

1 T. cumin seeds, crushed

¼ teas. ground allspice

½ teas. ground cinnamon

¼ teas. freshly-ground black pepper

½ teas. sea salt (opt.)

3 T. vegetable or olive oil

1 large onion, finely-diced

6-8 cloves of garlic, minced (to taste)

3 large carrots, finely-diced

3 large stalks celery, finely-diced

1 C. brown lentils, thoroughly rinsed and drained

6 C. vegetable stock

1 T. fresh lemon juice

1-2 T. honey (to taste)

Optional garnishes: Regular or vegan sour cream or yogurt, finely-chopped fresh parsley

In a small bowl or cup, combine herbs and spices and set aside.

In a large skillet or Dutch oven, heat oil over MEDIUM-HIGH heat. Add onion, garlic, carrots and celery and sauté for 2-3 minutes.

Stir in spice mix to coat vegetables evenly. Cover, reduce heat to MEDIUM and steam for 5 minutes to release flavours. Transfer to slow cooker. Add all remaining ingredients and stir to combine thoroughly.

Cook on HIGH for 3 ½ hours or LOW for 7 hours.

Adjust seasonings if required, garnish and serve.

Oven-Baked Chappatis

These tasty rounds can be filled with a variety of savory or sweet fillings, or good just on their own. Especially nice with **Fresh-Rosemary Hummus**. Makes 8 medium-chappatis.

1 C. unbleached white flour

½ C. whole wheat bread flour

1/3 C. melted butter or good-quality, non-whipped margarine

½ teas. sea salt

1 C. (approximately) buttermilk

Lightly grease a baking sheet and set aside.

Combine flours in a medium-sized mixing bowl. Add melted butter and salt and stir to combine. Gradually add just enough buttermilk to form a soft dough.

After kneading dough slightly on a floured board, form into a ball and allow to rest for 20 minutes, covered with a damp dish towel. Preheat oven to 350F while dough is resting.

Divide dough into 8 equal pieces and roll each into a small ball with your hands. On a floured board using a rolling pin, roll each ball into a circle about 6" in diameter.

Place rounds on prepared baking sheet, allowing a bit of space between each round.

Bake for 10 minutes then remove from oven and turn rounds. Bake 10 additional minutes until slightly browned.

Variations:

Whole-wheat: Use all whole-wheat bread flour for a chewier, denser texture.

Chick-pea flour: Substitute chick-pea flour for the ½ C. of whole wheat flour for a softer texture.

Sweet and Spicy Chili with Melt-In-Your-Mouth Cornbread Scones

Sweet and Spicy Chili

The spicy-sweet combination of flavours makes for an intriguing variation of this all-time family favorite. Satisfying and delicious; a meal in a bowl! Serves 6-8.

1 ½ -2 T. chili powder (to taste)

¼ teas. ground cloves

½ teas. ground cinnamon

1 T. cumin seeds, crushed

¼ teas. ground allspice

¼ teas. ground nutmeg

½ teas. ground ginger

1 T. crushed dried thyme leaves (to taste)

2 ½ C. precooked beans of choice: pinto, black, kidney... I

like to use a mixture of different types of beans for extra

colour and flavor.

49

2 T. vegetable oil

2 medium onions, chopped

4-6 cloves garlic, minced (to taste)

1 C. tomato salsa, mild or medium

2 T. tomato paste

1 vegetable soup cube, crumbled

$\frac{1}{4}$ -$\frac{1}{2}$ teas. **Tabasco** sauce (optional. if you like it HOT)

28 fl. oz. can beans in tomato sauce (use sauce too)

1 large green pepper, diced

2 C. kernel corn (thaw but don't pre-cook, before adding to chili, if using frozen corn)

Optional garnishes: Vegan or regular sour cream, chopped cilantro, shredded sharp Cheddar

In a small bowl or cup combine herbs and spices and set aside.

In a large skillet or Dutch oven, heat oil over MEDIUM-

HIGH heat. Sauté onions and garlic for 2 minutes. Add spice blend and stir to coat vegetables thoroughly. Cover, reduce heat to MEDIUM and steam for 5 minutes to release flavours. Transfer to slow cooker and add all remaining ingredients **except green pepper and corn.** Stir to combine thoroughly.

Cook on HIGH for 4 hours or LOW for 8 hours or until beans are very tender, **adding green pepper and corn** for last 20 minutes of cooking time on HIGH. Adjust seasonings if required, garnish and serve.

Variation: Omit canned beans in tomato sauce, increase precooked beans to 4 C. in total and add 1 additional cup of tomato salsa.

Melt-In-Your-Mouth Cornbread Scones

A perfect side for chili and all kinds of hearty soups. The
finer than cornmeal texture of the corn flour and creamed
corn result in a velvety crumb and delicious flavor.

Makes 8 large scones.

1 C. corn flour (organic, stone-ground if available)

1 ½ – 2 C. unbleached white flour (see instructions below)

2 teas. baking powder

½ teas. sea salt

½ C. chilled butter or good-quality, non-whipped margarine

10 fl. oz. can creamed corn

Lightly grease a baking sheet and set aside.

In a medium- sized bowl, combine dry ingredients. Start
with 1 ½ C. of the white flour. Cut in butter until crumbly.
Add cream corn and just enough of the remaining white
flour to form a soft dough. Form into a ball and allow to
rest 10 minutes on a floured board covered with a damp
dish towel.

While dough is resting, preheat oven to 375F.

Transfer dough ball to prepared baking sheet. Pat into a

circle about ¾- 1" thick. Score circle to form 8 triangles.

Bake for 20-25 minutes until a light golden brown. Reduce

heat to 350F after first 10 minutes of baking time if

browning too fast.

Variations:

Savory Cornbread Soup Scones: Add 1-2 T. crushed dried

thyme leaves or Italian seasoning blend with the dry

ingredients.

Poppy seed Cornbread Scones: Add 1 T. poppy seeds

with the dry ingredients.

Breakfast Cornbread Scones: Add 1-2 T. raw sugar with

the dry ingredients for a sweeter, breakfast scone. These are

wonderful with a dollop of blueberry or strawberry jam!

Dolce Vita Minestrone with Whole Wheat

Ricotta Scones

Dolce Vita Minestrone

Ah, the good life indeed! This classic soup never tasted

better. Add the **Whole Wheat Ricotta Scones** and a bottle

of Italian red wine and you're all set for a memorable

"urban peasant" feast! Serves 8.

3 T. olive oil

1 large onion, diced

4-6 cloves of garlic, minced (to taste)

4 large carrots, diced

4 large stalks of celery, diced

2 C. small cauliflower florets

1 ½ C. precooked navy beans

6C. vegetable soup stock

28 oz. can stewed tomatoes (with juice)

3T. red wine or white vinegar

2 teas. **Mrs. Dash Original Blend** seasoning

2 T. finely chopped fresh rosemary

½ -1 teas. sea salt (optional, to taste)

¼- ½ teas. freshly-ground black pepper (to taste)

2 large bay leaves (remove before serving)

1 T. honey or raw sugar (optional, if using tart tomatoes)

½ C. uncooked small pasta of choice (spirals, penne, shells…)

Optional garnish: Freshly-grated regular or vegan Parmesan cheese

In a large skillet or Dutch oven, heat olive oil over MEDIUM-HIGH heat. Add onions, garlic, carrots, celery and cauliflower (work in batches if necessary) and sauté for 3 minutes. Add Mrs. Dash seasoning, rosemary, salt and pepper and stir to combine thoroughly. Cover, reduce heat to MEDIUM and steam for 5 minutes to release flavors. Transfer to slow cooker. Add all remaining ingredients **except pasta.**

Cook on HIGH for 3 ½ hours or LOW for 7 hours **adding pasta** for last 30 minutes of cooking time on HIGH. Adjust seasonings if necessary. Garnish if desired and serve.

Whole Wheat Ricotta Scones

Hearty, savory scones with the subtle flavor of Ricotta

cheese. Quick to make and perfect with all kinds of soups.

Makes 8 large scones.

2 C. whole wheat pastry flour

2 teas. baking powder

$\frac{1}{2}$ teas. sea salt

4 T. chilled butter or good-quality, non-whipped margarine

1 large free-range egg

1 C. regular or light Ricotta cheese

$\frac{1}{4}$- $\frac{1}{2}$ C. table cream or soy creamer

Lightly grease a baking sheet and set aside.

In a medium bowl, combine flour, baking powder and salt.

Cut in butter until crumbly. In a small bowl or cup combine

remaining ingredients thoroughly and add to flour mixture.

Use your hands to combine all ingredients, adding a bit

more flour if necessary.

Knead slightly to form a soft but not sticky ball of dough.

Allow to rest on a floured board for 10-15 minutes, covered with a damp dish towel.

Preheat oven to 400F while dough is resting.

Transfer dough to prepared baking sheet. Pat into a circle about ¾- 1" thick. Score circle to form 8 triangles.

Bake for 20-25 minutes, reducing heat to 375F after first 10 minutes if browning too fast.

Extra Hearty Mac and Cheese with Garden Tomato Salsa

Extra Hearty Mac and Cheese

Another ultimate, comfort classic and even better from the slow cooker. KD's got nothing on this recipe! Serve with a generous dollop of **Garden Tomato Salsa** and vegetable of choice for a satisfying and delectable dinner. Serves 6.

450 grams uncooked small pasta of choice (bowties, wagon wheels, penne…)

3 T. butter or good-quality, non-whipped margarine

2 medium onions, diced

3 large stalks celery, diced

1 large sweet red or orange pepper, diced

3 T. unbleached white flour

2 teas. crushed dried thyme leaves

2 C. milk

10 oz. can reduced sodium (preferred) or regular cream of mushroom soup

2 T. Dijon mustard

2 C. grated sharp Cheddar cheese

¼- ½ teas. freshly-ground black or cayenne pepper (to taste)

1 teas. butter or margarine for greasing slow cooker liner

Optional Crunchy Parmesan Topping

1 ½ C. dried bread crumbs (a great way to use up day-old

bread)

½ C. finely grated Parmesan cheese

2 T. melted butter or good-quality non-whipped margarine

Optional garnish: Finely chopped fresh parsley

In a large cooking pot, cook pasta in a large quantity of

boiling salted water until al dente (slightly firm) about 5-6

minutes. Remove from heat, drain and set aside.

In the same pot used for cooking pasta (save dishes!) or a

large skillet, melt butter or margarine over MEDIUM-

HIGH heat. Add onions, celery and red pepper and sauté

for 5 minutes until slightly softened.

Reduce heat to MEDIUM, add flour and crushed thyme and stir to coat all vegetables thoroughly. Gradually add milk, stirring constantly until slightly thickened. Add mushroom soup, mustard, cheese and black pepper, continuing to stir constantly. Cook just until cheese is melted. Remove from heat.

Thoroughly grease the slow cooker liner with the 1 teas. of butter or margarine.

Pour in the pasta and sauce and stir to combine all ingredients thoroughly.

Cook on HIGH for 3 hours or LOW for 6 hours.

Optional Crunchy Parmesan Topping:

Combine topping ingredients in a small bowl. When mac and cheese has completed it cooking time, remove cover and evenly sprinkle crumb topping over the top. Using a conventional oven set on BROIL, place slow cooker under broiler element (**allow at least a couple of inches between slow cooker and heat source)** and broil just until topping is golden-brown and heated through. Be careful, this will only take a few minutes, **don't leave unattended**. Only add this step if you have an **oven-proof** slow cooker liner, check owner's manual! Remove from oven, garnish with parsley if desired and serve.

Garden Tomato Salsa

Bring a taste of summer to your table all winter long! This easy to make salsa is great on so many dishes: omelettes, wraps, with nachos and of course mac and cheese. You'll want to make several batches when garden tomatoes are at their peak. Makes 5- 1 pint jars.

6 C. chopped garden tomatoes (use juice too)

2 C. coarsely diced peppers of choice (use a combination of sweet and hot peppers, depending on your heat preferences)

4 medium onions, finely diced

½ C. white vinegar

½ C. raw brown sugar

1 teas. sea salt

3 T. pickling spice (tie in a muslin bag for easy removal)

Combine all ingredients in a large stock pot and bring to a boil. Reduce heat to LOW and simmer uncovered for 1 hour, stirring occasionally.

While salsa is cooking, prepare 5- 1 pint preserving jars

following label directions (Important: use new rings **every time**. The jars can be reused if properly sterilized each time).

Remove salsa from heat when cooking time is completed, removing spice bag.

Spoon salsa into prepared jars, wiping jar edges carefully, then seal.

Turn jars lid side down on a folded dry dish towel. After 24 hours, turn jars right side up and store in a cool, dark place for at least 2 weeks before serving. Will keep for several months.

After a jar is opened, store in refrigerator.

Spicy Cream of Carrot Soup with Simply the Best Cheddar Muffins

Spicy Cream of Carrot Soup

A great way to use up an abundance of carrots and get your daily requirements of vitamins A and C, in a yummy way! A carrot soup with a bit of a kick to it. It will warm you through and through. Serves 6.

½ - 1 T. crushed, dried thyme leaves (to taste)

½ teas. ground ginger

¼ teas. ground allspice

½ teas. ground nutmeg

2 teas. **Mrs. Dash Original Blend** seasoning (to taste)

¼ - ½ teas. freshly-ground black pepper (to taste)

½ teas. sea salt (opt.)

2 T. butter or good-quality non-whipped margarine

6 large or 8 medium carrots, diced

1 large onion, diced

4 cloves garlic, minced

1/3 C. uncooked long-grain brown rice

6 C. vegetable stock

½ C. soy milk or ½ C. vegan or regular sour cream (use sour cream for a rich, creamier soup)

Garnish: Finely chopped fresh parsley and/or thinly-sliced carrot circles

In a small bowl or cup, combine herbs and spices and set aside.

In a large skillet or Dutch oven, heat butter or margarine over MEDIUM heat. Add carrots, onion and garlic and sauté for 3 minutes. Add spice mix and stir to combine thoroughly. Cover and steam for 5 minutes to release flavours. Transfer to slow-cooker. Add all remaining ingredients **except soymilk or sour cream** and stir to combine thoroughly.

Cook on HIGH for 3 hours or LOW for 6 hours or until

rice is thoroughly cooked and carrots are soft but not

mushy, **adding soymilk or sour cream** for last 10 minutes

of cooking time on HIGH.

Remove from heat and allow to cool slightly.

Using an immersion blender, puree to desired consistency.

Garnish and serve.

Simply the Best Cheddar Muffins with Variations

These muffins have a wonderful flavor and texture. This is a

very popular recipe download at my cooking and craft blog:

Veggies, Yarns & Tails. Great with all kinds of soups,

stews, chili or on their own. Try one for breakfast with a

dollop of marmalade or strawberry preserves.

Makes 8 large muffins.

2 C. unbleached white flour

2 teas. baking powder

$\frac{1}{2}$ teas. sea salt

1 C. shredded sharp Cheddar cheese

1 C. milk

1 large free-range egg

$\frac{1}{4}$ C. vegetable or olive oil

Preheat oven to 400F.

Grease muffin tin or line with (look for unbleached) liners

and set aside.

In a medium-sized bowl combine the dry ingredients and

the shredded Cheddar. In a small bowl or large cup, combine remaining ingredients. Add to dry mixture just to combine, don't over mix.

Spoon batter into prepared muffin cups. Bake for 15-20 minutes until slightly golden on top and toothpick inserted in center of muffin comes out clean. Reduce heat to 375F after first 10 minutes if browning too fast.

Variations:

Cheddar Buttermilk: Substitute buttermilk for the milk for a slightly tangy muffin with a more biscuit-like texture. Also substitute 1 teas. baking soda and 1 teas. baking powder instead of the 2 teas. baking powder.

Herb Cheddar: Add a total of 1-2 T. dried or fresh herbs of choice: thyme, dill, chives, oregano...If using fresh herbs, chop finely before adding. Also add 1 teas. of **Mrs. Dash Original Blend** seasoning.

Swiss cheese: Substitute Swiss cheese for the Cheddar.

Berry Cheddar: Add ½ C. dried cranberries or dried blueberries to the dry ingredients.

Spicy Pepper Cheddar: Add ½ teas. cayenne pepper **or** 1 teas. chili powder and ½ C. finely diced red sweet pepper to the dry ingredients.

Whole Grain Cheddar: Substitute 1 C. whole wheat pastry flour for 1 C. of the white flour.

Poppy seed Cheddar: Add 1 T. poppy seeds to the dry ingredients.

German Sauerkraut Feast with Beet and Fresh Dill Layered Salad

German Sauerkraut Feast

Bring on Oktoberfest! Make this hearty and flavorful "feast" with minimal prep time and simple, pantry ingredients. Serve with **Beet and Fresh Dill Layered Salad** and with grainy mustard and/or sour cream on the side, for dipping sausages, if desired. This dinner just might change your mind about sauerkraut if it's been on your food "no list" previously. ;<) Serves 6.

1 teas. butter or margarine for greasing slow-cooker liner

10 medium red potatoes, peeled and quartered

1 T. dill or caraway seeds, your choice. (caraway has a stronger, distinctive flavor; the dill is slightly milder. Either one works well. Don't leave out!)

2 T. vegetable or olive oil

1 large onion, coarsely diced

4-6 cloves garlic, minced (to taste)

1 L. wine-type sauerkraut (use marinade too)

6 vegan beer-brat sausages, cut in 1" thick circles (I use **Tofurky** brand)

Thoroughly grease slow-cooker liner with butter or margarine and set aside.

In a large bowl, combine potatoes, dill or caraway seed and oil. Pour into slow-cooker, followed by layer of onions and then the minced garlic. Top with sauerkraut and marinade. Pour 1 C. water over all ingredients.

Cook on HIGH for 3 ½ hours or LOW for 7 hours or until potatoes are tender but not mushy **adding sausages** for last 15 minutes of cooking time on HIGH, layering on top of the sauerkraut.

Beet and Fresh Dill Layered Salad

A flavorful marinated salad, especially good to make when garden dill and beets are at their peak. Keeps for several days, covered in the refrigerator. A perfect side dish with all kinds of main dishes. Adds a brilliant color contrast on your plate too. Serves 6.

12 medium fresh (preferred) beets: precooked, peeled and cut into thin circles (or use whole canned beets, thoroughly rinsed and drained then sliced, in a pinch)

1 medium red Bermuda onion, thinly sliced in rings

3 T. chopped fresh dill-weed

Red Wine Marinade:

1/3 C. extra-virgin olive oil

5 T. red wine vinegar

1 teas. **Mrs. Dash Original Blend** seasoning

1 teas. sea salt

½ teas. freshly-ground black pepper

In a large bowl (that has a secure cover) layer 1/3 of the sliced beets, topped by ½ of the onion rings, then ½ of the dill-weed. Repeat layers, ending with the last 1/3 of the beets on top.

Combine marinade ingredients in a jar and shake thoroughly. Pour over vegetables, cover and refrigerate for at least 1 hour before serving.

Shake container gently to re-distribute marinade evenly before serving, especially if storing for a longer period of time.

"In the Navy" Bean Soup with Fresh Rosemary Hummus and Assorted Crackers

"In the Navy" Bean Soup

The name of this soup was inspired by a skit I saw, performed by one of my favorite comedians: Craig Ferguson, singing: "In the Navy". DO check it out on YouTube if you are in need of a LOL. And if it's a satisfying, sure to please dinner that you're thinking about right now, look no further than this recipe. Serves 6-8.

2 T. vegetable or olive oil

6-8 cloves of garlic, minced (to taste)

1 large onion, diced

3 large carrots, diced

3 large stalks celery, diced

2 medium potatoes, peeled and diced

1 T. crushed dried thyme leaves

½ - 1 teas. ground turmeric (to taste)

¼ - ½ teas. freshly-ground black pepper, to taste

½- 1 teas. sea salt, to taste (optional)

2 C. precooked navy beans

2 large bay leaves (remove before serving)

2 T. white or apple cider vinegar

1 vegan beer-brat sausage, finely diced (I use **Tofurky** brand)

6 C. vegetable soup stock

Optional garnish: Finely chopped fresh parsley

In a large skillet or Dutch oven, heat oil over MEDIUM-HIGH heat. Add vegetables and sauté for 3 minutes. Add spice mix and stir to combine thoroughly. Cover, reduce heat to MEDIUM and steam for 5 minutes to release flavours. Transfer to slow cooker. Add all remaining ingredients and stir to combine thoroughly.

Cook on HIGH for 4 hours or LOW for 8 hours or until

beans are tender but not mushy. Adjust seasonings if

required.

Garnish and serve.

Fresh Rosemary Hummus

A fresh take on traditional hummus! Rosemary adds a refreshing flavor boost to this oh-so-versatile spread. Try it on sandwiches, wraps, veggie burgers or with crunchy fresh veggies or crackers. Makes approximately 2 cups.

1 ½ C. precooked chickpeas (or use canned chickpeas in a pinch, thoroughly rinsed and drained)

4 T. fresh lemon juice

4 garlic cloves, chopped

1-2 T. light soy sauce (to taste)

2 T. olive oil (or a bit more if required, see instructions below)

½ C. tahini

2 teas. cumin seeds, crushed

1 T. chopped fresh rosemary

¼- ½ teas. cayenne pepper or **Tabasco** sauce, to taste

1 teas. **Mrs. Dash Original Blend** seasoning (optional)

Blend all ingredients in a food processor until smooth. Add a bit more olive oil or cold water if required, to blend easily, adding 1 T. at a time.

Adjust seasonings if required.

Chill in the refrigerator for at least 2 hours before serving to blend flavours.

Vegetable Curry with Rice and Red Lentil Salad

Vegetable Curry

Don't let your kids write off curry dishes until they've tried this one! Full of tasty, nutritious veggies with a "just right" spice blend. Good with Basmati or Jasmine rice or add the **Rice and Red Lentil Salad** and it's fancy enough when company is coming too. Serves 6-8.

2 T. good-quality regular curry powder or 1 T. Madras curry

1 T. cumin seeds, crushed

½ T. crushed, dried thyme leaves

¼ teas. ground allspice

1-2 teas. garam masala, to taste (optional)

¼ - ½ teas. freshly-ground black pepper, to taste

½ -1 teas. sea salt, to taste

3 T. vegetable or olive oil

1 T. minced fresh ginger-root

1 large onion, diced

4 large carrots, cut in ½" circles

2 C. small cauliflower florets

1 ½ C. precooked chickpeas

1 C. raisins

1 ½ C. vegetable soup stock

2 C. fresh or frozen cut green beans (if using frozen beans,
pour into a colander and partially thaw for about 30 minutes
before adding to recipe, don't precook)

1 large red sweet pepper, cut in thin strips

½ C. plain regular yogurt or sour cream

Garnish: 1 C. cashews, roughly chopped

In a small bowl or cup, combine herbs and spices and set
aside.

In a large skillet or Dutch oven, heat oil over MEDIUM-HIGH heat. Add ginger-root and sauté for 2 minutes to release flavor. Add all vegetables **except** red pepper and green beans and sauté for 3 minutes. Add spice blend and stir to coat vegetables evenly. Cover, reduce heat to MEDIUM and steam for 3 minutes to release flavours. Transfer to slow cooker. Add all remaining ingredients **except the green beans, red pepper and yogurt or sour cream.**

Cook on HIGH for 3 hours or LOW for 6 hours **adding the green beans** for last hour of cooking time. **Add the red pepper and yogurt or sour cream** for last 10 minutes of cooking time, on HIGH.

Adjust seasonings if required, garnish and serve.

Rice and Red Lentil Salad

A wonderful side dish for the **Vegetable Curry** and equally good as a salad with almost any meal. Makes a great potluck addition too. Colorful and refreshing. Serves 6-8.

½ C. uncooked red lentils, thoroughly rinsed and drained

1 large unpeeled red apple, diced

2 T. fresh lemon juice

4 C. precooked long-grain brown rice

½ C. raisins

½ C. salted or unsalted peanuts (optional)

½ C. hulled sunflower seeds

½ C. unsweetened, shredded coconut

1 T. finely-grated fresh ginger-root

Curry Yogurt Dressing:

½ C. regular plain yogurt

½ C. regular or light mayonnaise

½ -1 T. good quality regular curry powder or ¼ - ½ T. Madras curry powder

½ - 1 teas. sea salt (optional, to taste)

1-2 T. raw brown sugar (to taste, see method below)

2 T. tahini

In a small saucepan, combine lentils with just enough cold water to cover. Bring to a boil over MEDIUM heat. Reduce heat to LOW and simmer for 5-10 minutes just until water is absorbed, don't overcook. Remove from heat, fluff with a fork and set aside to cool.

In a large bowl, combine apple and lemon juice. Add remaining ingredients and gently toss to combine.

Whisk together dressing ingredients in a small bowl or cup. Adjust seasonings to taste, dressing should be tart, go easy on the brown sugar.

Chill salad and dressing in refrigerator until ready to serve. Drizzle salad with dressing, just before serving.

Cream of Rutabaga and Nutmeg Soup

with Sausage, Cheese and Thyme Muffins

Cream of Rutabaga and Nutmeg Soup

Don't write off rutabagas until you've tried this easy but
elegant, rich and creamy soup. The carrots add just a blush
of color. Quick to prepare and just plain good. Serves 6-8.

3 T. butter or good-quality non-whipped margarine

1 large (preferably sweet) onion, coarsely diced

8 C. diced rutabagas (these have a more intense flavor than
white turnips)

2 medium carrots, coarsely diced

½ teas. freshly grated nutmeg (use pre-ground nutmeg in a
pinch)

¼- ½ teas. freshly-ground black pepper (to taste

4 C. vegetable soup stock (add 1 additional cup if you like a thinner consistency of soup)

½ C. vegan or regular sour cream (light or regular)

Garnish: Finely chopped, fresh parsley

In a large skillet or Dutch oven, melt butter or margarine over MEDIUM-HIGH heat. Immediately add onions, carrots and rutabagas (work in batches if necessary) and sauté for 3 minutes. Cover, reduce heat to MEDIUM and steam for 5 minutes to release flavours. Transfer to slow cooker. Add all remaining ingredients **except sour cream** and stir to combine thoroughly.

Cook on HIGH for 3 ½ hours or LOW for 7 hours **adding sour cream** for last 10 minutes of cooking time, on HIGH. Remove from heat and allow to cool slightly.

Using an immersion blender, puree to desired consistency. Garnish and serve.

Sausage, Cheese and Thyme Muffins

A hearty and flavorful savory muffin. Colorful too!
Wonderful with cream soups of all kind: turnip, rutabaga,
carrot, potato...Or try one toasted in the morning for a
"breakfast-on-the-run", oh, so satisfying.

Makes 6 large or 8 regular muffins.

2 C. unbleached white flour

2 teas. baking powder

1 T. crushed dried thyme leaves

1 C. finely shredded "Sharp" cheese of choice: (Old

Cheddar or Swiss work well)

1 vegan beer brat sausage, finely diced (I use **Tofurky**

brand)

1 C. milk or soy milk

1 large free-range egg, beaten

¼ C. vegetable oil

Preheat oven to 400F.

Grease muffin tin or line with (look for unbleached) liners and set aside.

In a medium-sized bowl combine the dry ingredients with the shredded cheese and diced sausage.

In a small bowl or large cup, combine remaining ingredients.

Add to dry mixture just to combine, don't over mix.

Spoon batter into prepared muffin cups.

Bake for 20-25 minutes or until slightly golden on top and toothpick inserted in center of muffin comes out clean.

Reduce heat to 375F after first 10 minutes if browning too fast.

Hearty Baked Beans with Buttermilk and

Oatmeal Bread Machine Bread

Hearty Baked Beans

Another classic, family-favorite main dish. A wonderful aroma will fill your home while these tasty "bean beauties" simmer slowly to perfection. You might never settle for canned beans again! Serves 6.

2 T. vegetable oil

3 medium onions, coarsely diced

6 C. precooked navy beans

2 C. tomato sauce mixed with 1 C. water

2 T. grainy mustard

3 T. dark brown sugar

¼ C. molasses

2 vegan beer brat sausages, coarsely diced (I use **Tofurky** brand)

½ teas. cayenne pepper or Tabasco sauce

1 vegetable soup cube, crumbled

In a large skillet or Dutch oven, heat oil over MEDIUM-HIGH heat. Add onions and sauté for 3 minutes. Cover, reduce heat to MEDIUM and steam for 3 minutes, to soften slightly and release flavours.

Transfer to slow cooker. Add all remaining ingredients and stir to combine thoroughly.

Cook on HIGH for 5 hours or LOW for 10 hours or until beans are very tender but not mushy.

Add a bit more water or tomato sauce if required while beans are cooking.

Buttermilk and Oatmeal Bread Machine Bread

This bread has a wonderful texture and flavor. The buttermilk powder adds richness to the crumb. Excellent on its own or marvellous toasted!

1 ¼ C. boiling water

2 T. butter or good-quality non-whipped margarine

2 C. unbleached white flour

1 C. whole wheat or whole wheat blend flour

2 T. fructose, honey or raw sugar

1/3 C. regular rolled oats

4 T. buttermilk powder

1 teas. sea salt

1 ½ teas. Traditional dry yeast

In a small bowl, combine boiling water and butter or margarine. Set aside to cool to lukewarm.

In another bowl combine all remaining ingredients **except yeast**.

Add liquid and then dry ingredients to bread machine,

followed by the yeast (make sure not to get it wet).

Set at: WHOLE GRAIN/LIGHT or MEDIUM CRUST/1

½ POUNDS. Start machine.

Allow loaf to cool slightly before removing from pan when

baking is completed.

Tangy Split Pea Soup with Quick and Easy

Vegan Soup Biscuits

Tangy Split Pea Soup

This soup is especially good on a cold fall or winter day.

Packed with nutritious vegetables and satisfying split peas. A

meal in a bowl! Serves 6-8.

3 T. vegetable or olive oil

1 large onion, diced

4-6 cloves garlic, minced (to taste)

4 large carrots, diced

4 large stalks celery, diced

1 vegan beer- brat sausage, finely diced (I use **Tofurky**

brand)

2 C. yellow or green split peas, thoroughly rinsed and

drained

7 C. vegetable stock

2 large bay leaves (remove before serving)

10 black peppercorns (remove before serving) (if possible, put in a small muslin/cooking bag for easy removal)

2 T. Dijon mustard

2 teas. **Mrs. Dash Original Blend** seasoning (optional)

Garnishes: Grated fresh carrot and/or finely-chopped fresh parsley

In a large skillet or Dutch oven, heat oil over MEDIUM-HIGH. Add onion, garlic, carrots and celery and sauté for 3 minutes. Cover, reduce heat to MEDIUM and steam for 5 minutes to release flavours. Transfer to slow cooker. Add all remaining ingredients and stir to combine thoroughly.

Cook on HIGH for 4 hour or LOW for 8 hours.

Garnish and serve.

Quick and Easy Vegan Soup Biscuits with Variations

These quick and easy biscuits have a wonderful texture and are great with all kinds of soups, stews, and chili. Or try them filled with scrambled eggs and toppings of choice for hearty breakfast biscuits. Makes 6 large or 8 regular biscuits.

1 C. unbleached white flour

1 C. whole wheat pastry flour

2 teas. baking powder

½ teas. sea salt

4 T. good quality non-whipped margarine (I use **Earth Balance Organic)**

3/4 C. (approximately) soy milk

Combine flours, baking powder and sea salt in a medium sized bowl. Cut in margarine until mixture has a coarse mealy texture. Gradually add just enough soy milk to form a ball of dough; use your hands but don't overwork dough.

Add a bit more flour if necessary.

Allow dough to rest in a warm place for 10 minutes, covered with a damp dish towel.

While dough is resting, preheat oven to 400F. Lightly grease a baking sheet and set aside.

Roll out dough to approximately 3/4" thickness. Using a round or square cutter or a large coffee mug (dip in flour first) cut out biscuits and place on prepared baking sheet. Bake 12-15 minutes until slightly golden brown. Reduce heat to 375 after first 5 minutes if browning too fast.

Variations:

Non-vegan, cheese: Add 1 C. finely grated hard cheese of choice with the dry ingredients. Also substitute butter for margarine and dairy milk for soy milk, if desired.

Tea: Add 2 T. raw sugar with the dry ingredients. Also add 1 C. currants or raisins and a ½ teas. of ground cinnamon, if desired.

Herb: Add 1-2 T. dried crushed dried herbs of choice (thyme, savory, basil...) with the dry ingredients.

Whole Grain: Substitute all whole wheat pastry flour instead of the white and whole wheat.

Moroccan Vegetable Stew with Fragrant Orange Basmati Rice

Moroccan Vegetable Stew

Comfort food with a kick! If you love yams, you will love this hearty, colorful stew with an intriguing blend of spices. Serve with **Fragrant Orange Basmati Rice** for a special treat. A perfect main dish when company is coming too.

Serves 6.

1-2 teas. ground turmeric (to taste)

1 teas. ground cumin

½ teas. cayenne pepper

1 teas. ground cinnamon

¼ teas. ground nutmeg

2 teas. **Mrs. Dash Original Blend** seasoning

2 T. vegetable oil

1 large onion, diced

4-6 cloves garlic, minced (to taste)

4-5 medium yams (3- 3 ½ pounds in total) cut in 1" cubes

4 large carrots, diced

1 C. vegetable stock

1 C. precooked chickpeas

15 oz. can diced or stewed tomatoes with juice

1 C. raisins

2 bay leaves (remove before serving)

3-4 T. regular or vegan sour cream

In a small bowl or cup, combine spices and set aside.

In a large skillet or Dutch oven, heat vegetable oil over
MEDIUM-HIGH heat. Add onions and garlic and sauté for
3 minutes. Add spice mix and stir to combine ingredients
thoroughly. Cover, reduce heat to MEDIUM and steam for
5 minutes to release flavours. Transfer to slow cooker and

add all remaining ingredients **except sour cream**. Stir to combine thoroughly.

Cook on HIGH for 3 hours or LOW for 6 hours or until vegetables are all tender but not mushy, **adding sour cream** for last 10 minutes of cooking time on HIGH. Adjust seasonings if required and serve.

Note: Cooking times for yams can vary a bit, depending on the variety you are using.

Fragrant Orange Basmati Rice

A perfect rice side dish that's good with all kinds of main dishes especially the **Moroccan Vegetable Stew** and spicy curries. Colorful, with a wonderful fragrance and flavor.

Serves 6.

2 T. vegetable or olive oil

4 C. precooked basmati rice (preferably brown)

4 T. fresh orange juice

zest of one large navel orange

½ teas. ground coriander

4 T. finely chopped fresh parsley

In a large skillet, heat oil over MEDIUM-HIGH heat. Add rice and sauté for 3 minutes. Add all remaining ingredients and continue to sauté for 2 more minutes, just to heat through.

Remove from heat and serve immediately.

The Best Veggie Beet Borscht with Rye and Fennel Seed Bread Machine Bread

The Best Veggie Beet Borscht

Add a slice of freshly-baked: **Rye and Fennel Seed Bread** and a dollop of sour cream for a "peasant- food" feast your whole family will love. Loaded with nutritious veggies too! Serves 6.

3 T. vegetable or olive oil

1 large onion, diced

4-6 cloves garlic, minced (to taste)

3 large carrots, diced

3 large stalks celery, diced

2 medium potatoes, peeled and diced

2 C. shredded red or green cabbage

1 beer-brat vegan sausage, finely diced (I use **Tofurky** brand)

5 C. vegetable soup stock

1-2 T. honey (to taste)

2-3 T. red wine or white vinegar (to taste)

28 oz. can diced tomatoes, with juice (or equivalent fresh, chopped tomatoes with juice)

1 T. dill seed, crushed

2 teas. **Mrs. Dash Original Blend** seasoning

2 large bay leaves (remove before serving)

¼ - ½ teas. sea salt (to taste, optional)

¼ - ½ teas. freshly-ground black pepper (to taste)

3 C. precooked, diced fresh beets (or equivalent whole canned beets: rinsed, drained and diced)

2 T. cornstarch

Optional garnish: Regular or vegan sour cream

In a large skillet or Dutch oven, heat oil over MEDIUM-HIGH heat. Add onion, garlic, carrots, celery, potatoes and cabbage (work in batches if necessary) and sauté for 3 minutes. Cover, reduce heat to MEDIUM and steam for 5 minutes to release flavours. Transfer to slow cooker. Add all remaining ingredients **except beets and cornstarch** and stir to combine thoroughly.

Cook on HIGH for 3 ½ hours or LOW for 7 hours, **adding beets** for last hour of cooking time.

Combine **cornstarch with ¼ C. of cold water and add for last 10 minutes** of cooking time on HIGH. Adjust seasonings if required.

Garnish if desired and serve.

Rye and Fennel Seed Bread Machine Bread

A hearty, fragrant loaf. Perfect with all kinds of soup; especially beet borscht. The fennel seeds add a wonderful and distinctive flavor. Excellent for toast or toasted sandwiches too (try Swiss cheese… extra-yummy good!)!

1 C. boiling water

2 T. butter or good-quality non-whipped margarine

2 T. molasses

1 T. fresh lemon juice

1 C. light or medium rye flour

3 C. unbleached white flour

1 teas. sea salt

2 T. raw sugar

1-2 T. fennel seeds (start with 1 T. Fennel has a strong flavor; add more the next time if desired)

2 teas. Traditional dry yeast

½ C. sunflower seeds (optional)

In a small bowl, combine boiling water, butter, molasses and

lemon juice. Set aside to cool to lukewarm.

In another bowl combine remaining ingredients **except the**

yeast and sunflower seeds.

Add liquid and then dry ingredients to bread machine,

followed by the yeast (make sure not to get it wet).

Set at: BASIC/LIGHT or MEDIUM CRUST/ 2 POUNDS.

Start machine. **Add sunflower seeds** at beep, if using.

Allow loaf to cool slightly before removing from pan when

baking is completed.

Old-Fashioned "Meaty" Stew with Parsley Dumplings

This truly is a meal-in-a-pot; no other side dishes required.
Even confirmed beef-stew lovers will enjoy this tasty,
satisfying redo. It's time for the Chuck wagon to move
on. ;<)

Note: Allow a bit of prep time for last hour before serving,
to complete this recipe, see method.

Serves 6.

3 T. vegetable oil

2 medium onions, coarsely diced

4 large or 6 medium carrots, cut in 1" circles

6 medium potatoes, peeled and quartered

2 C. diced rutabagas

$\frac{1}{4}$ - $\frac{1}{2}$ teas. freshly-ground black pepper (to taste)

2 teas. **Mrs. Dash Original Blend** seasoning

4 T. unbleached white flour

3 C. vegetable soup stock

4 commercial veggie "beef-style" burgers (approximately
250-285 grams in total) cut in 1" cubes (if using from
frozen, partially thaw before using- just enough to be able to
cut burgers into cubes)

6 T. Worcestershire sauce

1 C. frozen baby peas

Parsley Dumplings

1 ½ C. unbleached white flour

2 teas. baking powder

½ teas. sea salt

¼ teas. freshly-ground black pepper (optional)

3 T. finely chopped fresh parsley

1/3 C. chilled butter or good-quality non-whipped

margarine

½ - ¾ C. milk or soy milk (as required)

In a large skillet or Dutch oven, heat oil over MEDIUM-HIGH heat. Add onions, carrots, potatoes and rutabagas (work in batches if necessary) and sauté for 3 minutes. Stir in black-pepper and Mrs. Dash seasoning. Cover, reduce heat to MEDIUM and steam for 5 minutes to release flavors. Transfer to slow cooker.

Stir in flour and dredge vegetables evenly. Add vegetable soup stock and stir to combine all ingredients thoroughly.

Cook on HIGH for 3 ½ hours or LOW for 7 hours peas **adding prepared veggie burgers and frozen peas** for last 30 minutes of cooking time on HIGH. You will also be **adding dumplings** at the same time.

While stew is cooking, in a shallow dish, combine veggie burger cubes with Worcestershire sauce. Refrigerate and allow to **marinate for 1 hour.**

Thaw frozen peas for 30 minutes before adding to stew.

40 minutes before cooking time is completed, prepare:

Dumplings:

In a medium bowl, combine dry ingredients, including salt

and pepper (if using). Cut in butter or margarine until

mixture is crumbly. Add parsley and stir to combine

thoroughly. Gradually add just enough milk to form a soft

dough. Don't over-mix.

After adding prepared veggie burger chunks and peas to

stew and stirring to combine thoroughly, drop heaping

spoonfuls of dumpling dough around outer edges of slow

cooker (make about 6-8 dumplings) to top stew. **Work as**

quickly as possible to retain cooking temperature.

Cover and cook stew with dumplings for remaining 30

minutes of cooking time on HIGH or until dumplings are

puffed and fully cooked.

Variations:

Buttermilk Dumplings: Use buttermilk instead of milk or soy milk. Substitute 1 teas. baking soda and 1 teas. baking powder for the 2 teas. of baking powder.

Herb Dumplings: Substitute 1 T. crushed, dried thyme leaves for the fresh parsley.

Stay tuned for the next volume of:

The Groovy Green Kitchen

Simply, Super Supper Soups

Enjoy a sample recipe now!

Summer's Bounty Herb and Veggie Soup

During the summer, enjoy all the "fruits of your labor" those amazing garden veggies and herbs.

This luscious soup is a great way to use lots of "green wonders" when they are at their peak.

Do use vegetables and herbs from your own garden if at all possible for maximum freshness or check out the organic offerings at a local farmer's market or grocery store.

Makes 4-6 servings

2 T. olive oil

1 medium sweet onion, diced

4 medium carrots, diced

1 medium zucchini, diced (scrubbed and unpeeled if garden fresh)

4 medium garden tomatoes, chopped (use the juice too) or 15 oz. can stewed or diced tomatoes

1 ½ C. precooked beans of choice: kidney, fava, cannellini, pinto, or a combination of your favs. Use canned, drained and rinsed beans in a pinch.

3 T. uncooked long-grain brown rice (thoroughly rinsed and drained)

3 T. pot or pearl barley (thoroughly rinsed and drained)

4 C. vegetable soup stock

2 T. apple cider vinegar

½ -1 T. raw sugar or honey (to taste)

3 bay leaves (remove before serving)

1-2 T. chopped fresh or 1-2 teas. crushed dried thyme (to taste)

1-2 T.chopped fresh or 1-2 teas.crushed dried oregano (to taste)

1 teas. Chinese 5 Spice seasoning

sea salt and black pepper, to taste

1 medium green or sweet red pepper, diced

1 C. fresh or frozen baby peas

Optional garnishes: Finely chopped flat leaf parsley and/or freshly-grated regular or vegan Parmesan cheese

In a large soup pot, heat olive oil over MEDIUM-HIGH heat. Add onions, carrots and zucchini and sauté for 3 minutes. Cover, reduce heat to LOW and steam for 3 additional minutes to release flavors.

Add all remaining ingredients **except green/red pepper and peas** and bring to a boil.

Cover, reduce heat to LOW and simmer for 30-40 minutes, just until barley and rice are both cooked. **Add peppers and peas** for last 15 minutes of cooking time.

Add a bit more stock or water if necessary, if soup is thicker than you like.

Adjust seasonings if required.

Garnish and serve.

***

If you enjoyed this book, a review at Amazon.com would be most appreciated! :<)

Made in the USA
Lexington, KY
26 August 2013